HOMES IN THE WILDERNESS

A PILGRIM'S JOURNAL OF PLYMOUTH PLANTATION IN 1620

by William Bradford and Others
of the Mayflower Company

edited by Margaret Wise Brown

illustrated by Mary Wilson Stewart

PURPLE HOUSE PRESS
Kentucky

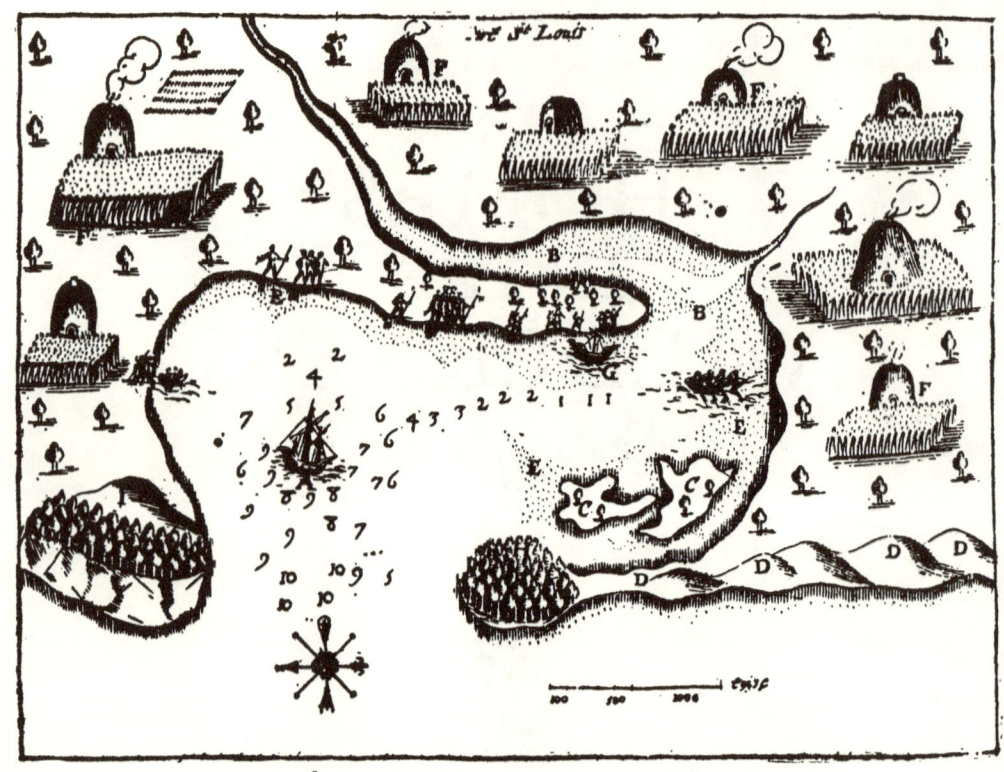

CHAMPLAIN'S MAP OF PLYMOUTH HARBOR IN 1605

Published by
Purple House Press
PO Box 787
Cynthiana, Kentucky 41031

Classic Living Books for Kids and Young Adults
purplehousepress.com

Written by William Bradford and others in 1620 and 1621
Edited by Margaret Wise Brown in 1939
Illustrated by Mary Wilson Stewart in 1939
Cover map of New England in 1685 from the David Rumsey Map Collection
This edition, cover design and arrangement © 2022 by Purple House Press

ISBN 979-8-88818-010-5

EDITOR'S NOTE

Homes in the Wilderness was first published at London in 1622 as *A Relation or Journal of the Proceedings of the Plantation settled at Plymouth in New England*. The book is commonly called *Mourt's Relation* because the preface is signed *G. Mourt.*, and no other indication of authorship is given. There was, however, no such person as Mourt or Morton among the Mayflower's company, and it is now believed that Governor Bradford, Edward Winslow, and others of the colonists kept this journal.

For this edition the old language has been somewhat modernized, but every effort has been made to preserve the flavor of the original vigorous King James English. The book has been retitled *Homes in the Wilderness* because the old title is unwieldy and fails to suggest the dramatic struggle of this gallant company of a hundred who made their homes in the wilderness.

THE MAYFLOWER'S PASSENGERS

John Carver (8).
    Catherine, his wife.
    Desire Minter.
    John Howland, } men-
    Roger Wilder, } servants.
    William Latham, } boys.
    Jasper More,   }
    A maid-servant.

William Bradford (2).
    Dorothy, his wife.

Edward Winslow (5).
    Elizabeth, his wife.
    George Soule, } men-
    Elias Story,   } servants.
    Ellen More.

William Brewster (6).
    Mary, his wife.
    Love,   } sons.
    Wrestling,   }
    Richard More, } boys.
    —— More,   }

Isaac Allerton (6).
    Mary, his wife.
    Bartholomew, }
    Remember,   } children.
    Mary,   }
    John Hooke, boy.

Miles Standish (2).
    Rose, his wife.

John Alden (1).

Samuel Fuller (1). [His servant, William Butten, died at sea.]

Christopher Martin (4).
    ——, his wife.
    Solomon Prower, } men-
    John Langemore, } servants.

William Mullins (5).
    ——, his wife.
    Joseph,   } children.
    Priscilla, }
    Robert Carter, servant.

William White (5).
 Susanna, his wife.
 Resolved, son.
 William Holbeck, } men-
 Edward Thomson, } servants.

Richard Warren (1).

Stephen Hopkins (8).
 Elizabeth, his wife.
 Giles,
 Constance, } chil-
 Damaris, } dren.
 Oceanus, born at sea.
 Edward Doten, } men-
 Edward Leister, } servants.

Edward Tilley (4).
 Ann, his wife.
 Henry Samson, } children in
 Humility Cooper, } their care.

John Tilley (3).
 ——, his wife.
 Elizabeth, daughter.

Francis Cook (2).
 John, his son.

Thomas Rogers (2).
 Joseph, his son.

Thomas Tinker (3).
 ——, his wife.
 ——, son.

John Ridgdale (2).
 Alice, his wife.

Edward Fuller (3).
 Ann, his wife.
 Samuel, son.

John Turner (3).
 ——, } sons.
 ——,

Francis Eaton (3).
 Sarah, his wife.
 Samuel, son.

James Chilton (3).
 ——, his wife.
 Mary, daughter.

John Crackstone (2).
 John, his son.

John Billington (4).
 Ellen, his wife.
 John, } sons.
 Francis,

Moses Fletcher (1).

John Goodman (1).

Digory Priest (1).

Thomas Williams (1).

Gilbert Winslow (1).

Edmond Margeson (1).

Peter Brown (1).

Richard Britteridge (1).

Richard Clark (1).

Richard Gardiner (1).

John Allerton (1).

Thomas English (1).

LIST OF OLD WORDS AND THEIR MEANINGS

ado: commotion
anon: immediately
antic: clown
base: a small cannon about four and one-half feet long
beck: stream
betimes: early
broach: a spit or spike for holding roasting meat over a fire
compassed: encircled
ell: about a yard
fain: forced
fathom: a man's arm spread or six feet
fowling piece: shotgun for shooting fowl
furlong: a furrow's length or an eighth of a mile
furniture: equipment
hart: deer
helving: putting wooden handles on metal tools
impaled: surrounded by a stockade
Irish trousers: long, tight-fitting trousers
league: about three miles
let: hinder
listed: liked
matches: slow-burning fuses for setting off matchlock guns

minion: a great gun or cannon, seven or eight feet long
neat: cow
occasionally: accidentally
pale board: stockade post
piece: gun
plain: level
pole: sixteen and a half feet
presently: immediately
rand: strip
rive: split
saker: a great gun or cannon, eight or ten feet long
seat: settle
seethe: boil
snaphance: a kind of gun
sounded: swooned, fainted
spit's depth: depth of the blade of a shovel
squibs: paper rolled up around gunpowder, to make a homemade firecracker
towards: near at hand, advancing
truck: trade
want: lack
whelmed: turned upside down
wood gale: bayberry

Publisher's note: Divers is not a misspelling of diverse—it is a word in its own right, meaning an unspecified quantity when used before a plural noun.

HOMES
IN THE
WILDERNESS

September 6, 1620. Wednesday, the wind coming E.N.E. a fine small gale, we loosed from Plymouth, having been kindly entertained and courteously used by divers friends there dwelling.

November 9th. After many difficulties in boisterous storms, at length by God's good providence we espied land, which by break of the day we deemed to be Cape Cod. And so afterward it proved. The appearance of it much comforted us, especially seeing so goodly a land and wooded to the brink of the sea. It caused us to rejoice together and praise God that had given us once again to see land.

And thus we made our course S.S.E., purposing to go to a river ten leagues to the south of the Cape. But at night, the wind being contrary, we put round again for Cape Cod Bay.

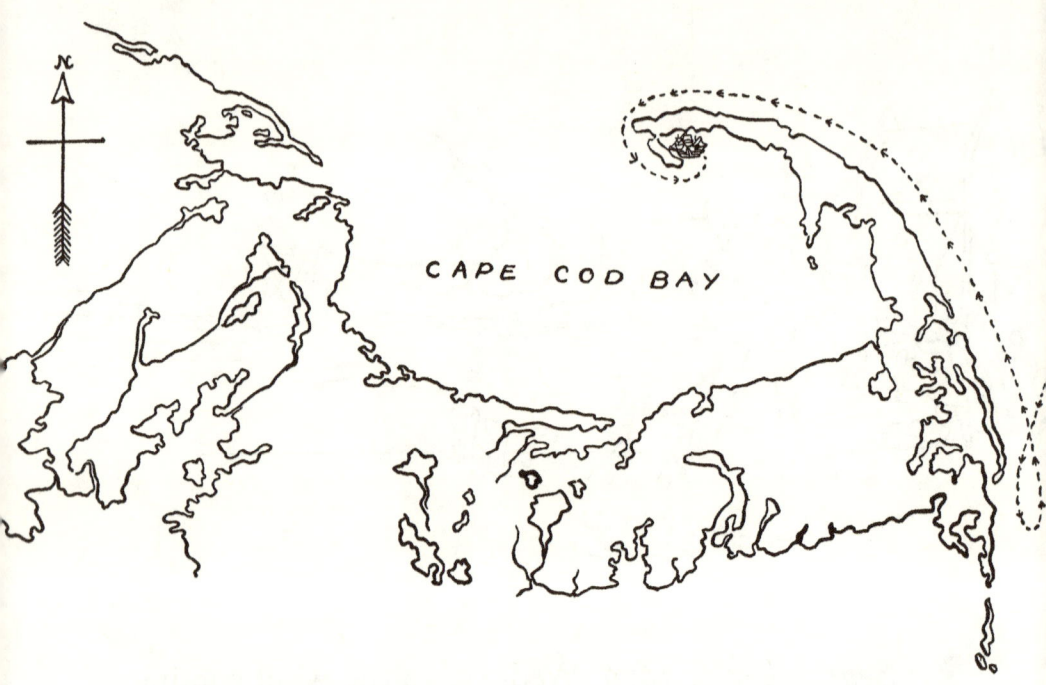

November 11th. We came to an anchor in the bay, which is a good harbor and pleasant bay about four miles over from land to land, wherein a thousand sail of ships may safely ride. It is circled round except in the entrance and compassed about to the very sea with oaks, pines, juniper, sassafras, and other sweet wood. There we relieved ourselves with wood and water and refreshed our people, while our shallop was fitted to coast the bay in search of an habitation. There was the greatest store of fowl that ever we saw.

And every day we saw whales playing hard by us in that place. Had we had instruments and means to take them (which to our great grief we wanted) we might have made a very rich return. Our master and his mate and others experienced in fishing professed we might have made three or four thousand pounds' worth of oil.

They preferred it before Greenland whale-fishing and purpose to fish for whale here the next winter. For cod we essayed but found none, though no doubt there is good store in their season; neither got we any fish all the time we lay there but some few little ones on the shore. We found great mussels, very fat and full of sea pearl, but we could not eat them. They made us all sick that did eat, sailors as well as passengers, causing us to cast and scour. But all were soon well again.

The bay is so round and circling that before we could come to anchor we went round all the points of the compass. We could not come near the shore by three quarters of an English mile because of shallow water. This was a great prejudice to us, for our people going on shore were forced to wade a bowshoot or two in going a-land, which caused many to get colds and coughs, for it was freezing cold weather.

This day before we came to harbor, observing that some were not well affected to unity and concord but gave appearance of faction, it was thought good that there should be an association and agreement, so that we should combine together in one body and submit to such government and governors as we should by common consent agree to make and choose. We therefore set our hands to this that follows word for word.

In the name of God Amen. We whose names are underwritten, the loyal Subjects of our dread sovereign Lord, King James, by the grace of God of Great Britain, France, *and* Ireland *King, Defender of the Faith, &c.*

Having undertaken for the glory of God, and advancement of the Christian Faith, and honor of our King and Country, a Voyage to plant the first Colony in the Northern parts of Virginia, *do by these presents solemnly and mutually in the presence of* God *and one of another, covenant and combine ourselves together into a civil body politic for our better ordering and preservation, and furtherance of the ends aforesaid; and by virtue hereof to enact, constitute, and frame such just and equal Laws, Ordinances, acts, constitutions, & offices from time to time as shall be thought most meet and convenient for the general good of the Colony; unto which we promise all due submission and obedience. In witness whereof we have hereunder subscribed our names at* Cape Cod, *the 11th of* November, *in the year of the reign of our sovereign Lord, King* James, *of* England, France, *and* Ireland *the 18th and of* Scotland *the 54th,* Anno Domino *1620.*

The same day, so soon as we could, we set ashore fifteen or sixteen men, well armed. With them we sent some to fetch wood, for we had none left, and also to see what the land was and what inhabitants they could meet with. They found it to be a small neck of land; on the side where we lay is the bay and on the further side the sea. The ground or earth is sand hills like the downs in Holland but much better, the crust of the earth being excellent black earth for a spit's depth. It is all wooded with oaks, pines, sassafras, juniper, birch, holly, vines, some ash, and walnut. The wood for the most part is open and without underwood, fit either to go or ride in. At night our people returned but found not any person nor habitation. They laded their boat with juniper, which smelled very sweet and strong. This we burnt the most part of the time we lay there.

November 13th. Monday, we unshipped our shallop and drew her on land to mend and repair her, having been forced to cut her down in bestowing her betwixt the decks. She was much opened with the people's lying in her, which kept us long there, for our carpenter made slow work of it. It was sixteen or seventeen days before he had finished her. Our people went on shore to refresh themselves and our women to wash, as they had great need.

But whilst we lay thus still, some of us, impatient of delay, desired for our better furtherance to travel by land into the country to see whether it might be fit for us to seat in or no. This was not without appearance of danger, not having the shallop nor means to carry provision but on our backs. The willingness of the persons to go was liked, but because of the danger the thing itself was rather permitted than approved.

So with cautions, directions, and instructions, sixteen men were set out, with every man his musket, sword and corslet under the conduct of Captain Miles Standish, unto whom were adjoined for counsel and advice, William Bradford, Stephen Hopkins, and Edward Tilley.

November 15th. Wednesday, we were set ashore. When we had ordered ourselves in the order of a single file and marched about the space of a mile by the sea, we espied five or six people with a dog coming towards us. First, we supposed them to be Master Jones, since he and some of his men were ashore and knew of our coming. But when they saw us they ran into the wood and whistled the dog after them, and so we knew them to be savages.

We marched after them into the woods, lest other Indians should lie in ambush. But when the Indians saw our men following them, they ran away with might and main. Our men turned out of the wood after them, for it was the way they intended to go, but they could not come near them. We followed them that night about ten miles by the trace of their footings and saw how they had come the same way they went. At a turning we perceived how they ran up an hill to see whether we followed them.

At length night came upon us, and we were constrained to take up our lodging, so we set forth three sentinels, and some of the rest fetched wood while others kindled a fire, and there we held our rendezvous for the night.

November 16th. In the morning, as soon as we could see the trace, we proceeded on our discovery and had the track until we had compassed the head of a long creek. There they took into another wood and we after them, supposing to find some of their dwellings. We marched under hills and valleys through boughs and bushes which tore and ripped our very armor in pieces, and yet could meet with none of them. Nor did we see their houses nor find any fresh water, which we greatly desired and stood in need of, for we brought neither beer nor water with us. Our only victuals were biscuit and Holland cheese and a little bottle of *aqua vitae*, so that we were sore athirst.

About ten o'clock we came into a deep valley, full of brush, wood gale, and long grass, through which we found little paths or tracks, and there saw a deer. There we found springs of fresh water, of which we were heartily glad, and sat us down and drunk our first New England water with as much delight as ever we drunk drink in all our lives. When we had refreshed ourselves, we directed our course full south that we might come to

the shore, which a short while after we did. There we made a fire, that they in the ship might see where we were (as we had direction to do). And so we marched on towards that place where, as we sailed into the harbor, there had seemed to be a river opening itself into the mainland.

As we went into a valley, we found a fine clear pond of fresh water about a musket shot broad and twice as long. There grew much sassafras and many small vines, and fowl and deer haunted there. From here we marched on and found about fifty acres of ground fit for the plow, and some signs where the Indians had formerly planted their corn. After this some thought it best to go down and travel on the sea-sands. By this means some of our men were tired and lagged behind, so we stayed and gathered them up and struck into the land again.

There we found a little path to certain heaps of sand, one whereof was covered with old mats. It had a wooden thing like a mortar whelmed on the top of it and an earthen pot laid in a little hole at the end thereof. Musing what it might be, we digged and found a bow and, as we thought, arrows, but they were rotten. We supposed there were many other things, but because we deemed them graves we put in the bow again and made it up as it was, leaving the rest untouched. We thought it would be odious unto them to ransack their sepulchers. We went on further and found new stubble of which they had gotten corn this year, many walnut trees full of nuts, great store of strawberries, and some vines.

Passing thus a field or two which were not great, we came to another of which corn had also been new gotten. There we found where an house had been and four or five old planks laid together. Also we found a great kettle, which had been some ship's kettle and brought out of Europe. There was also an heap of sand made like the former, but it was newly done, for we could see how they

had paddled it with their hands. This we digged up, and in it we found a little old basket full of fair Indian corn. We digged further and found a fine great new basket full of very fair corn of this year with some thirty-six goodly ears, some yellow, some red, and others mixed with blue, which was a very goodly sight. The basket was round and narrow at the top and was very handsomely and cunningly made. It held about three or four bushels, which was as much as two of us could lift up from the ground.

Whilst we were busy about these things, we set our men sentinels in a round ring, all but two or three who digged up the corn. We were in suspense what to do with it and the kettle. At length after much consultation we concluded to take the kettle and as much of the corn as we could carry away with us. And when our shallop came, if we could find any of the people and come to parley with them, we would give them the kettle again and satisfy them for their corn. So we took all the ears and put a good deal of the loose corn in the kettle for two men to bring away on a staff. Besides, they that could put any into their pockets filled the same. The rest we buried again, for we were so laden with armor that we could carry no more.

Not far from this place we found the remainder of an old fort or palisade, which, as we conceived, had been made by some Christians. This was also hard by that place which we thought had been a river, unto which we went. We found it so to be, divided into two arms by an

high bank standing right by the mouth. That which was next unto us was the less, the other arm being more than twice as big and not unlikely as an harbor for ships. But whether it be a fresh river or only an indraught of the sea, we had no time to discover, for we had commandment to be out but two days. Here also we saw two canoes, one on one side, the other on the other side. We could not believe it was a canoe, till we came near it.

So we returned, leaving the further discovery hereof to our shallop, and came that night back again to the fresh water pond. There we made our rendezvous that night, making a great fire and a barricade to windward of us, and kept good watch with three sentinels all night, every one standing when his turn came while five or six inches of match was burning. It proved a very rainy night.

November 17th. In the morning we took our kettle and sunk it in the pond and trimmed our muskets, for few of them would go off because of the wet. We coasted the wood again to come home, in which we were shrewdly puzzled and lost our way. As we wandered we came to a tree where a young sprout was bowed down over a bow with some acorns strewed underneath. Stephen Hopkins said it had been set to catch some deer. So, as we were looking at it, William Bradford, who had been in the rear, came up also and looked upon it. And as he went about it, it gave a sudden jerk up, and he was immediately caught by the leg. It was a very pretty device, made with a rope of their own making, which we brought away with us. It had a noose as artfully made as any roper in England can make and as like ours as can be.

In the end we got out of the wood and were fallen about a mile too high above the creek. There we saw three bucks, but we would rather have had one of them. We also sprung three couple of partridges, and as we came along by the creek we saw great flocks of wild geese and ducks, but they were very fearful of us. So we marched some while in the woods, some while on the sands, and other while in water up to the knees, till at length we came near the ship. And then we shot off our pieces and the long boat came to fetch us. Master Jones and Master Carver, being on the shore with many of our people, came to meet us.

And thus we came both weary and welcome home, and delivered in our corn into the store to be kept for feed, for we knew not how to come by any. And therefore were we very glad, purposing so soon as we could meet with any of the inhabitants of that place to make them large satisfaction. This was our first discovery.

Whilst our shallop was repairing, our people did make things as fitting as they could and time would, seeking out wood, helving tools, and sawing timber to build a new shallop. But the discommodiousness of the harbor did much hinder us, for we could neither go to nor come from the shore but at high water. This was much to our hindrance and hurt, for oftentimes we waded to the middle of the thigh and oft to the knees to go and come from land. Some did it necessarily and some for their

own pleasure, but, the weather proving suddenly cold and stormy, it brought to the most, if not to all, coughs and colds which afterward turned to the scurvy, whereof many died.

November 27th. When our shallop was fit (indeed before she was fully fitted, for there was two days' work bestowed on her after), some twenty-four men of our own were appointed and armed to go and make a more full discovery of the rivers before mentioned. Master Jones was desirous to go with us and took such of his sailors as he thought useful for us, so we were in all about thirty-four men. We made Master Jones our leader, for we thought it best herein to gratify his kindness and forwardness.

When we were set forth it proved rough weather and cross winds. We were constrained, some in the shallop and others in the long boat, to row to the nearest shore the wind would suffer us to go unto and then to wade out above the knees. The wind was so strong that the shallop could not keep to the water and was forced to harbor there that night. But we marched six or seven miles further and appointed the shallop to come to us as soon as it could. It blowed and did snow all that day and night and froze withal. Some of our people that are dead took the original of their death here.

November 28th. The next day about eleven o'clock our shallop came to us and we shipped ourselves. The wind being good, we sailed to the river we formerly discovered, which we named Cold Harbor. When we came to it, we found it not navigable for ships, yet we thought it might be a good harbor for boats, for it flows there twelve foot at high water. We landed our men between the two creeks and marched some four or five miles by the greater of them, and the shallop followed us.

At length night grew on, and our men were tired with marching up and down the steep hills and deep valleys, which lay half a foot thick with snow. Master Jones, wearied with marching, was desirous we should take up our lodging, though some of us would have marched further. So we made there our rendezvous for that night under a few pine trees. As it fell out we got three fat geese and six ducks to our supper, which we ate with soldiers' stomachs, for we had eaten little all that day. Our resolution was to go up to the head of this river the next morning, for we supposed it would prove fresh water.

November 29th. But in the morning our resolution held not, because many liked not the hilliness of the soil and badness of the harbor. So we turned towards the other creek that we might go over and look for the rest of the corn that we left behind when we were there before. When we came to the creek, we saw the canoe lying on the dry ground and a flock of geese in the river. One made a shot at them and killed a couple, and we launched the canoe and fetched them. When we had done, she carried us over, seven or eight at once.

This done, we marched to the place where formerly we found the corn, which place we called Corn-hill. There we digged and found the rest, of which we were very glad. We also digged in a place a little further off and found a bottle of oil. We went to another place, which we had seen before, and digged and found more corn, *viz.* two or three baskets full of Indian corn, a bag full of their beans, and a good many fair ears of corn. Whilst some of us were digging this up, some others found another heap of corn, which they digged up also, so that we had in all about ten bushels, which will serve us sufficiently for feed.

And sure it was God's good providence that we found this corn, for else we know not how we should have done, for we knew not how we should find or meet with

any of the Indians, except it be to do us a mischief. Also we had never in all likelihood seen a grain of it if we had not made our first journey; for the ground was now covered with snow and hard frozen. We were fain to hew and carve the ground a foot deep with our cutlasses and short swords, and then wrest it up with levers, for we had forgot to bring other tools.

Whilst we were at this employment, foul weather being towards, Master Jones was earnest to go aboard, but sundry of us desired to make further discovery and to find out the Indians' habitations. So we sent home with him our weakest people and some that were sick, and all the corn. Eighteen of us stayed still and lodged there that night and desired that the shallop might return to us next day and bring some mattocks and spades with them.

November 30th. The next morning we followed certain beaten paths and tracks of the Indians into the woods, supposing they would have led us to some town or houses. After we had gone a while, we came upon a very broad beaten path, well nigh two foot broad. We lighted all our matches and prepared ourselves, concluding we were near their dwellings. But in the end we found it to be only a path made to drive deer in when the Indians hunt, as we supposed.

When we had marched five or six miles into the woods and could find no signs of any people, we returned again another way. As we came into the plain ground we found a place like a grave, but it was much bigger and longer than any we had yet seen. It was also covered with boards. We mused what it should be and resolved to dig it up. There we found first a mat, and under that a fair bow, and then another mat, and under that a board about three quarters of a yard long, finely carved and painted, with three tines or broaches on the top like a crown. Also between the mats we found bowls, trays, dishes, and such like trinkets.

At length we came to a fair new mat, and under that two bundles, one bigger and the other less. We opened the greater and found in it a great quantity of fine and perfect red powder. In that were the bones and skull of a man. The skull had fine yellow hair still on it, and some of the flesh was unconsumed. There was with it a knife, a pack-needle, and two or three old iron things. It was bound up in a sailor's canvas shirt and a pair of cloth breeches. The red powder was a kind of embalmment and yielded a strong but not offensive smell. It was as fine as any flour.

We opened the less bundle likewise and found some of the same powder in it and the bones and head of a little child. About the legs and other parts of it were bound strings and bracelets of fine white beads. There was also by it a little bow about three quarters of a yard long and some other odd knacks. We covered the corpse up again and brought sundry of the prettiest things away with us. After this we digged in sundry like places but found no more corn nor anything else but more graves.

There was a variety of opinions amongst us about the embalmed person. Some thought it was an Indian lord and king; others said the Indians all have black hair and never any was seen with brown or yellow hair. Some thought it was a Christian of special note who had died amongst them, and they buried him thus to honor him. Others thought they had killed him and had done it in triumph over him.

Whilst we were thus ranging and searching, two of the sailors, who were newly come on the shore, by chance espied two houses which were lately dwelt in, but the Indians were gone. They, having their pieces and hearing nothing, went into the houses and took out some things but durst not stay. They came and told us; so some seven or eight of us went back with them and found out how we had gone within a slight shot of them before.

The houses were made with long young sapling trees, so that both ends stuck into the ground. They were made round like unto an arbor and covered down to the ground with thick and well-wrought mats. The door was not over a yard high, made of a mat to open. The chimney was a wide open hole in the top, which they had a mat to cover when they pleased. One might stand and go upright in them. In the midst of them were four little stakes knocked into the ground and small sticks laid over, on which they hung their pots and what they had to seethe. Round about the fire they lay on mats, which are their beds. The houses were double-matted, for as they were matted without so were they within with newer and fairer mats.

In the houses we found wooden bowls, trays and dishes, earthen pots, hand baskets fashioned of crab shells wrought together, also an English pail or bucket. It wanted a handle, but it had two iron ears. There were

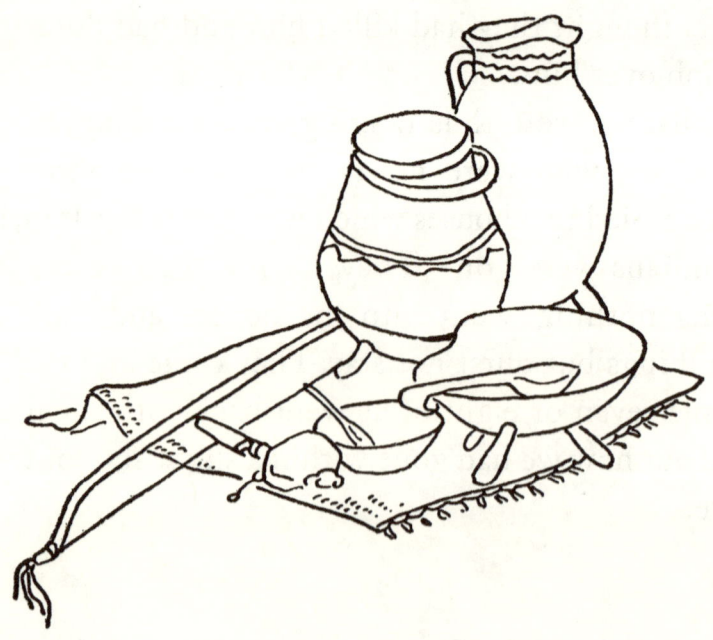

also baskets of sundry sorts, some bigger and some lesser, some finer and some coarser, and some curiously wrought with black and white in pretty works. And there was sundry other of their household stuff. We found two or three deer's heads, one whereof had been newly killed, for it was still fresh. There was a company of deer's feet

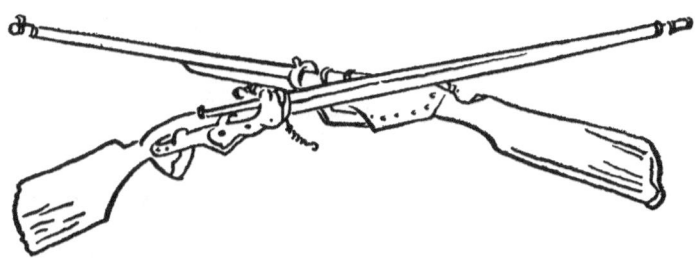

stuck up in the houses, harts' horns and eagles' claws and sundry such like things, also two or three baskets full of parched acorns, pieces of fish, and a piece of a broiled herring. We found a little silk grass and tobacco seed with some other seeds which we knew not.

Without were sundry bundles of flags and sedge, bulrushes, and other stuff to make mats. Thrust into an hollow tree were two or three pieces of venison, but we thought it fitter for the dogs than for us. Some of the best things we took away but left the houses as they were.

So, it growing towards night and the tide being almost spent, we hasted down to the shallop and got our things aboard that night. We had intended to have brought some beads and other things to have left in the houses in sign of peace and to show that we meant to truck with them, but it was not done because of our hasty coming away from Cape Cod. But so soon as we can meet conveniently with them, we will give them full satisfaction. Thus much of our second discovery.

Having thus discovered this place, it was controversial amongst us what to do touching our abode and settling there. Some thought it best for many reasons to abide there.

First, there was a convenient harbor for boats, though not for ships.

Secondly, good corn ground was ready to our hands, as we saw by experience in the goodly corn it yielded, which would again agree with the ground and would be natural feed for the same.

Thirdly, Cape Cod was like to be a place of good fishing, for we saw daily great whales of the best kind for oil and bone come close aboard our ship and in fair weather swim and play about with us. Once when the sun shone warm there was one who came within half a musket shot of the ship and lay for a good while above water as if she had been dead. Two prepared to shoot at her to see whether she would stir or no. He that gave fire first, his musket flew in pieces both stock and barrel, yet thanks be to God neither he nor any man else was hurt with it, though many were there about. But when the whale saw her time she gave a snuff and away.

Fourthly, the place was likely to be healthful, secure, and defensible.

But the last and especial reason was that now the heart of winter and unseasonable weather was come upon us. We could not go upon coasting and discovery without danger of losing men and boat, especially considering what variable winds and sudden storms do there arise. Upon this would follow the overthrow of all. Also

cold and wet lodging had so tainted our people (scarce any of us were free from vehement coughs) that if they should continue long in that estate it would endanger the lives of many and breed diseases and infection amongst us.

Again, we had yet some beer, butter, flesh, and other such victuals left, which would quickly be all gone. Then we should have nothing left to comfort us in the great labor and toil we were like to undergo at the first. It was also conceived that whilst we had competent victuals the ship would stay with us, but when these grew low they would be gone and let us shift as we could.

Others, again, greatly urged going to Agawam, a place twenty leagues off to the northwards, which they had heard to be an excellent harbor for ships, better ground, and better fishing.

Secondly, for anything we knew there might be hard by us a far better seat, and it would be a great hindrance to seat in a place from which we would remove again.

Thirdly, the water was but in ponds, and it was thought there would be none in summer or very little.

Fourthly, the water there must be fetched up a steep hill.

But to omit many reasons and replies used hereabouts, it was in the end concluded to make some discovery within the bay, but in no case so far as Agawam. Besides, Robert Coppin, our pilot, made relation of a great navigable river and good harbor in the headland of this bay in which he had been once. It was almost right over

against Cape Cod, being in a right line not much above eight leagues distant. Because one of the wild men with whom they had some trucking stole a harpoon iron from them, they called it Thievish Harbor. Beyond that place they were enjoined not to go. Whereupon a company was chosen to go out upon a third discovery.

Whilst some were employed in this last discovery, it pleased God that Mistress White was brought to bed of a son, who was called Peregrine.

December 6th. This day, through God's mercy, we escaped a great danger by the foolishness of a boy, one of Francis Billington's sons. In his father's absence from the ship he had got a little barrel half full of gunpowder and scattered it in and about their cabin. He had made squibs and shot off a piece or two, and, there being a charged fowling piece, he had shot her off in the cabin. The fire came within four foot of the bed between the decks. There were many flints and iron things about the cabin and many people about the fire and yet by God's mercy no harm done.

December 6th. Wednesday, it was resolved our discoverers should set forth, for the day before was too foul weather. And so they did, though the day was almost over ere all things could be ready. Ten of our men were appointed who were of themselves willing to undertake it, to wit: Captain Standish, Master Carver, William Bradford, Edward Winslow, John Tilley, Edward Tilley, John Howland, and three of London, Richard Warren, Stephen Hopkins, and Edward Doten, and two of our seamen, John Allerton and Thomas English. Of the ship's company there went two of the master's mates. Master Clarke and Master Coppin, the master gunner, and three sailors. The narration of this discovery follows, penned by one of the company.

December 6th. Wednesday, we set out in very cold and hard weather. After we launched from the ship we were a long while before we could get clear of a sandy point, which lay within less than a furlong of the same. In this time two were sick, and Edward Tilley had like to have sounded with cold. The gunner was also

sick unto death (hope of trucking led him to go) and so remained all that day and night. At length we cleared the point and got up our sails. Within an hour or two we got under the weather shore and then had smoother water and better sailing. It was very cold, for the water froze onto our clothes, making them many times like coats of iron.

We sailed six or seven leagues by the shore but saw neither river nor creek. But at length we met with a tongue of land with a sandy point flat off from the shore. We bore up to gain the point and found there a fair income or road of a bay, being a league across at the narrowest and some two or three leagues in length. But we made right over to the land before us and left the discovery of this income till the next day. As we drew near to the shore, we espied some ten or twelve Indians very busy about a black thing. What it was we could not tell. Afterwards they saw us and ran to and fro as if they had been carrying some thing away. We landed a league or two from them and had much ado to put ashore anywhere, it lay so full of flat sands. When we came to shore, we made us a barricade and got firewood and set out our sentinels and betook us to our lodging, such as it was. We saw the smoke of the fire which the savages made that night about four or five miles from us.

December 7th. In the morning we divided our company, leaving some eight in the shallop. The rest on the shore went to discover this place but found it only to be a bay without either river or creek coming into it. Yet we deemed it to be as good a harbor as Cape Cod, for they that sounded it found a ship might ride in five fathom water. We on the land found it to be level soil but none of the fruitfullest. We saw two streams of fresh water. These were the first running streams we saw in this country, but one might stride over them.

We found also a great fish called a grampus dead on the sands. They in the shallop found two of them also in the bottom of the bay, dead in like sort. They were cast up at high water and could not get off for the frost

and ice. They were some five or six paces long with about two inches of fat, fleshed like a swine. They would have yielded a great deal of oil, if there had been time and means to have taken it. So, finding nothing for our turn, both we and the shallop returned. We then directed our course along the sea-sands to the place where we first saw the Indians. When we were there, we saw that it was a grampus which they had been cutting up. They had cut it into long rands or pieces about an ell long and two handfuls broad. Here and there we found a piece scattered by the way, as it seemed for haste. This place the most were minded we should call Grampus Bay because we found so many of them there.

We followed the track of the Indians' bare feet a good way on the sands, until at length we saw where they struck into the woods by the side of a pond. As we went to view the place, one said he thought he saw an Indian house among the trees, so we went up to see. Here we and the shallop lost sight one of another till night, it being now about nine or ten o'clock. So we lighted on a path, but saw no house, and followed a great way into the woods. At length we found where corn had been set, but not that year.

Anon we found a great burying place, one part whereof was encompassed with a large palisade like a churchyard, with young saplings four or five yards long, set two or three foot in the ground as close by one another as they could. Within it was full of graves, some bigger and some less. Some were also paled about, and others had like an Indian

house made over them, but not matted. These graves were more sumptuous than those at Corn-hill, yet we digged none of them up, but only viewed them and went our way. Without the palisade were graves also, but not so costly.

From this place we went and found more corn ground, but not of this year. As we ranged we lighted on four or five Indian houses which had been lately dwelt in, but they were uncovered and had no mats on them. Otherwise they were like those we found at Corn-hill but had not been so lately dwelt in. Nothing was left but two or three pieces of old mats and a little sedge. A little further on we found two baskets full of parched acorns hid in the ground, which we supposed had been corn when we began to dig the same. We cast earth thereon again and went our way. All this while we met with none of their people.

We went ranging up and down hill till the sun began to draw low, and then we hasted out of the woods that we might come to our shallop. When we were out of the woods, we espied it a great way off and called them to come unto us. So being both weary and faint, for we had eaten nothing all that day, we fell to making our rendezvous and getting firewood, which always cost us a great deal of labor. By the time we had done and our shallop had come to us, it was within night. They feared because they had not seen us in so long a time, thinking we would have kept by the shoreside. We fed upon such victuals as we had and, after we had set our watch, betook us to our rest.

About midnight we heard a great and hideous cry, and our sentinel called *Arm, Arm*. So we bestirred ourselves and shot off a couple of muskets, and the noise ceased. We concluded that it was a company of wolves or foxes, for one told us he heard such a noise in New-found-land.

December 8th. About five o'clock in the morning we began stirring, and two or three who doubted whether their pieces would go off or no made trial of them and shot them off, but thought nothing of it. After prayer we prepared ourselves for breakfast and for a journey, and, it being now the twilight in the morning, it was thought meet to carry the things down to the shallop. Some said it was not best to carry armor down; others said it would then be readier. Two or three said they would not carry theirs till they went themselves, but mistrusted nothing at all. As it fell out, the water not being high enough, they laid the things upon the shore and came up to breakfast.

Anon, all of a sudden, we heard a great and strange cry, which we knew to be the same voices, though they varied their notes. One of our company being abroad came running in and cried, *They are men! Indians! Indians!* And withal, their arrows came flying amongst us.

Our men ran out with all speed to recover their arms, as by the good providence of God they did. In the meantime, Captain Miles Standish, having a snaphance ready, made a shot. Another shot after him. After they two had shot, another two of us were ready, but he wished us not to shoot until we could take aim, for we knew not what need we should have. There were only four who had their arms ready. We stood before the open side of our barricade which was assaulted, for we thought it best to defend it lest the enemy should take it and our stuff and so have the more vantage against us.

Our care was no less for the shallop, but we hoped the rest would defend it. We called unto them to know how it was with them, and they answered, *Well, well, everyone, and be of good courage.* We heard three of their pieces go off, and the rest called for a firebrand to light their matches. One took a log out of the fire on his shoulder and went and carried it unto them, which was thought did not a little discourage our enemies. The cry of our enemies was dreadful, especially when our men ran out to recover their arms. Their note was after this manner, *Woath woach ha ha hach woach*. Our men were no sooner in arms but the enemy was ready to assault them.

There was a lusty man and no whit less valiant, who was thought to be their captain and who stood behind a tree within half a musket shot of us and there let his arrows fly at us. He was seen to shoot three arrows which were all voided. He at whom the first arrow was aimed saw it and stooped down and it flew over him. The rest were avoided also. He stood three shots of a musket, but at length one took full aim at him, after which he gave an extraordinary cry and away they went all.

We followed them about a quarter of a mile, leaving six to keep our shallop, for we were careful of our business. Then we shouted all together two several times and shot off a couple of muskets and so returned. This we did that they might see we were not afraid of them nor discouraged.

Thus it pleased God to vanquish our enemies and give us deliverance. By their noise we could guess that they were not less than thirty or forty, though some thought that they were many more yet. In the dark of the morning we could not so well discern them among the trees as they could see us by our fireside. We took up eighteen of their arrows, which we have sent to England by Master Jones. Some of them were headed with brass, others with harts' horn, and others with eagles' claws. Many more no doubt were shot, for these we found were almost covered with leaves. Yet by the especial providence of God none of them either hit us or hurt us, though many came close by us and on every side of us, and some coats which hung up in our barricade were shot through and through. So after we had given God thanks for our deliverance, we took our shallop and went on our journey. We called this place the first encounter.

From hence we intended to have sailed to the aforesaid Thievish Harbor, if we found no convenient harbor by the way. Having the wind good, we sailed all the day along the coast about fifteen leagues but saw neither river nor creek to put into. After we had sailed an hour or two, it began to snow and rain and to be bad weather. About the midst of the afternoon the wind increased and the seas began to be very rough. The hinges of the rudder broke, so that we could steer no longer with it, but two men with much ado were fain to serve with a couple of oars. The seas were grown so great that we were much troubled and in great danger, and night grew on.

Anon Master Coppin bade us be of good cheer for he saw the harbor. As we drew near, the gale being stiff and we bearing great sail to get in, we split our mast in three pieces and were like to have cast away our shallop. Yet by God's mercy recovering ourselves, we had the flood with us and struck into the harbor.

Now he that thought this had been the place was deceived, for it was a place where not any of us had been before. Coming into the harbor he that was our pilot did bear up, which had cast us away if he had continued. Yet still the Lord kept us, for we bore up toward an island before us, and gained the lee of this island. Being compassed about with many rocks and dark night growing upon us, it pleased the divine providence that we fell upon a place of sandy ground upon a strange island, where our shallop did ride safe and secure all that night. We kept our watch all night in the rain upon that island.

December 9th. In the morning we marched about it and found no inhabitants at all. Here we made our rendevous all that day, being Saturday.

December 10th. On the Sabbath day we rested.

December 11th. On Monday we sounded the harbor and found it a very good harbor for our shipping. We marched also into the land and found divers corn fields and little running brooks, a place very good for situation. So we returned to our ship again with the good news to the rest of our people, which did much to comfort their hearts.

December 15th. We weighed anchor to go to the place we had discovered. Coming within two leagues of the land, we could not fetch the harbor but were fain to put about again towards Cape Cod, our course lying W. and the wind at the N.W.

December 16th. But it pleased God that the next day, being Saturday, the wind came fair, and we put to sea again and came safely into a safe harbor. Within half an hour the wind changed, so that if we had been letted but a little, we had gone back to Cape Cod.

This harbor is a bay greater than Cape Cod. It is in fashion like a sickle or fishhook and compassed with a goodly land. In the bay are two fine islands, uninhabited, wherein is nothing but wood, oaks, pines, walnut, beech, sassafras, vines, and other trees which we know not. This bay is a most hopeful place with innumerable store of excellent good fowl, and there cannot but be

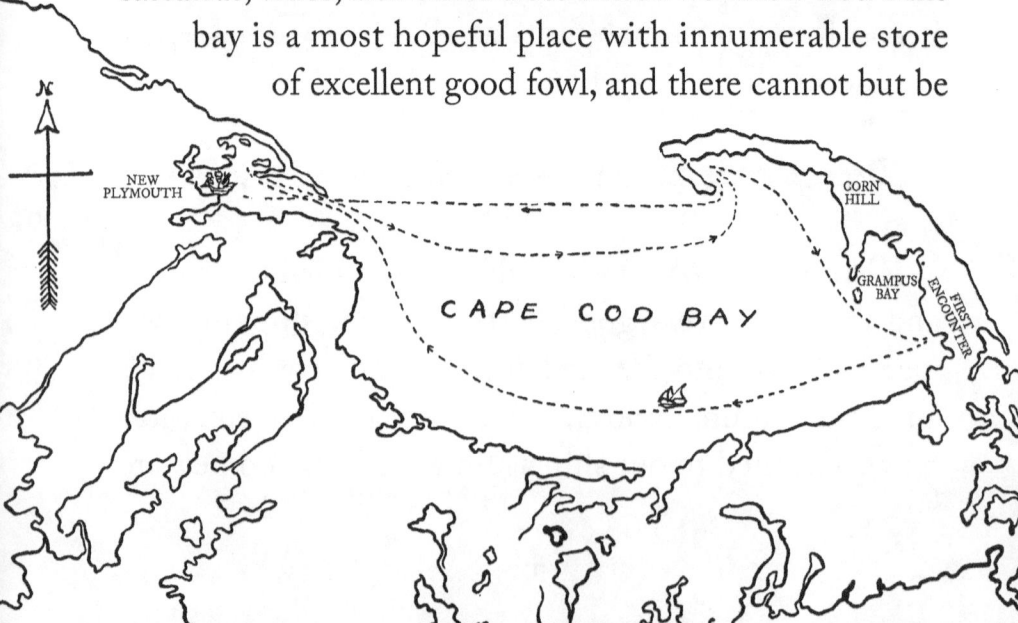

fish in their seasons. Skate, cod, turbot, and herring we have tasted of. There is also abundance of mussels, the greatest and best that ever we saw, and crabs and lobsters in their time infinite.

December 18th. Monday, we went a-land, manned with the master of the ship and three or four of the sailors and marched along the coast in the woods some seven or eight miles. We found where formerly had been some inhabitants and where they had planted their corn, but saw not an Indian nor an Indian house. We found no navigable river but saw four or five small running brooks of very sweet fresh water that all run into the sea. The crust of the earth is excellent black mold for a spit's depth, and more in some places. There are two or three great oaks but not very thick, pines, walnuts, beech, ash, birch, hazel, holly, asp, sassafras in abundance, vines everywhere, cherry trees, plum trees, and many others which we know not.

Many kinds of herbs we found here in winter: strawberry leaves innumerable, sorrel, yarrow, chervil, brook-lime, liverwort, water-cress, great store of leeks and onions, and an excellent strong kind of flax, and hemp. Here is sand, gravel, and excellent clay, no better in the world, excellent for pots and will wash like soap, and great store of stone, though somewhat soft. The best water that ever we drunk is here, and the streams now begin to be full of fish. That night, many of us being weary with marching, we went aboard again.

December 19th. The next morning, being Tuesday, we went forth again to discover further, some on the land and some in the shallop. The land we found as before. We saw a creek and went up three English miles, a very pleasant river. At full sea, a bark of thirty ton may go up, but at low water scarce our shallop could pass.

We had a great liking to plant in this place but that it is so far from our fishing, our principal profit. It is likewise so encompassed with woods that we should be in much danger of the savages. Our number being so little and there being so much ground to clear, we thought good to quit that place till we were of more strength.

Some of us having a good mind to plant in the greater isle for safety, we crossed the bay, which is there five or six miles over, and found the isle about a mile and a half or two miles about. There was no fresh water but two or three pits, so that we doubted of fresh water in summer, and it was so full of wood that we could hardly clear so much as to serve us for corn. Besides we judged it cold for our corn, and some parts very rocky. Yet divers thought of it as a place defensible and of great security. That night we returned again aboard ship, with resolution to decide on some of those places the next morning.

December 20th. So in the morning, after we had called on God for direction, we came to this resolution: to go presently ashore again and to take a better view of the two places which we thought most fitting for us. We could not now take time for further search or consideration, our victuals being much spent, especially our beer. After our landing and viewing of the places, so well as we could we came to a conclusion by most voices to settle on the mainland. It was at the first place on an high ground where there is a great deal of land cleared which had been planted with corn three or four years ago. There is a very sweet brook that runs under the hillside and many delicate springs of as good water as can be drunk. It is a place where we may harbor our shallops and boats

exceeding well. In this brook there is much good fish in their seasons, and on the further side of the river also is much corn ground cleared.

In one field is a great hill, on which we point to make a platform and plant our ordinance, so that it will command the land all round about. From thence we may see across the bay to Cape Cod and far out into the sea. Our greatest labor will be the fetching of our wood, which is half a quarter of an English mile away, but there is enough so far off. What people inhabit here we yet know not, for as yet we have seen none. So there we made our rendezvous and a place for some of our people, about twenty, resolving in the morning for all of us to come ashore and build houses.

December 21st. But the next morning, being Thursday, it was stormy and wet, so that we could not go ashore. Those that remained there all night were wet but could do nothing, not having daylight enough to make them a sufficient guard house to keep them dry. All that night it blew and rained extremely. It was so tempestuous that the shallop could not go to land so soon as was meet, for they had no victuals on land. With much ado about eleven o'clock the shallop went off with provision, but could not return. It blew so strong and was such foul weather that we were forced to let fall our anchor and ride with three anchors to an head.

December 22nd. Friday, the storm still continued so that we could not get a-land, nor they come to us aboard. This morning goodwife Allerton was delivered of a son, but dead born.

December 23rd. Saturday, so many of us as could went on shore and felled and carried timber to provide ourselves stuff for building.

December 24th. Sunday, our people on shore heard a cry of some savages, as they thought, which caused an alarm. They stood on their guard expecting an assault, but all was quiet.

December 25th. Monday, we went on shore, some to fell timber, some to saw, some to rive, and some to carry. No man rested all that day. But towards night some, as they were at work, heard a noise of some Indians, which caused us all to go to our muskets. But we heard no further, so we came aboard again and left some twenty to keep the guard house. That night we had a sore storm of wind and rain.

It being Christmas day, we began by drinking water aboard, but at night the master caused us to have some beer. So on board we had now and then some beer, but on shore they had none at all.

December 26th. Tuesday, it was such foul weather that we could not go ashore.

December 27th. Wednesday, we went to work again.

December 28th. On Thursday, so many as could went to work on the hill, where we purposed to build a platform for our ordinance. This hill commands all the plain and also the bay, and from there we may see far into the sea. Two rows of houses and a fair street might there be easier impaled than on flat ground.

So in the afternoon we went to measure out the

48

ground. First we took notice how many families they were. All the men who had no wives were ordered to join with some family, as they thought fit, so that we might build fewer houses. This was done, and we reduced them to nineteen families. To greater families we allotted larger plots, to every person half a pole in breadth and three in length. And so lots were cast where every man should lie and the plots staked out.

We thought this proportion was large enough at the first for houses and gardens which were to be impaled around, considering the weakness of our people. Many of them were growing ill with colds, for our former discoveries in frost and storms, and the wading ashore at Cape Cod had brought much weakness amongst us, which increased every day more and more, and after was the cause of many of their deaths.

December 29th & 30th. Friday and Saturday, we fitted ourselves for our labor, but our people on shore were much troubled and discouraged with rain and wet these days, it being very stormy and cold. We saw great smokes of fire made by the Indians, about six or seven miles from us as we conjectured.

January 1, 1621. Monday, we went betimes to work. We were much hindered in lying so far off shore and fain to go as the tide served, so that we lost much time. Our ship drew so much water that she lay almost a mile and a half off, though a ship of seventy or eighty ton at high water may come to the shore.

January 3rd. On Wednesday some of our people being abroad to gather thatch, they saw great fires of the Indians. Our people went to the corn fields yet saw no savages.

January 4th. Thursday, Captain Miles Standish with four or five more went to see if they could meet with any of the savages in that place where the fires were made. They went to some of their houses, but these were not lately inhabited, and they could not meet with any. As they came home they shot at an eagle and killed her, which was excellent meat. It was hardly to be discerned from mutton.

January 5th. Friday, one of the sailors found alive upon the shore an herring, which the master had to his supper. This put us in hope of fish, for as yet we had got but one cod, as we wanted small hooks.

January 6th. Saturday, Master Martin was very sick with no hope of life, to our judgment. So Master Carver was sent for to come aboard to speak with him about his accounts. He came the next morning.

January 8th. Monday, was a very fair day, and we went betimes to work. Master Jones sent the shallop as he had formerly done to see where fish could be got. They had a great storm at sea and were in some danger, but at night they returned with three great seals and an excellent good cod which did assure us of plenty of fish shortly.

This day, Francis Billington, having the week before seen from the top of a tree on an high hill a great sea, as he thought, went with one of the master's mates to see it. They went three miles and then came to a great water, divided into two great lakes. The bigger of them is five or six miles in circuit and in it is an isle of a cable's length square. The other is three miles in compass. In their estimation they

are fine fresh water, full of fish and fowl. A brook issues from it. It will be an excellent help for us in time. They found seven or eight Indian houses, but not lately inhabited. When they saw the houses they were in some fear, for they were but two persons and one piece.

January 9th. Tuesday, was a reasonable fair day, and we went to labor that day in the building of our town in two rows of houses for more safety. We divided by lot the plot of ground whereon to build our town after the proportion formerly allotted. We agreed that every man should build his own house, thinking by that course men would make more haste than working in common. The common house, in which for the first we made our rendezvous, was near finished and wanted only covering, it being about twenty foot square. Some made mortar and some gathered thatch, so that in four days half of it was thatched. Frost and foul weather hindered us much. This time of the year we seldom could work half the week.

January 11th. Thursday, William Bradford, being at work for it was a fair day, was vehemently taken with a grief and pain, and so shot to his hip bone that it was doubted he would live. He got cold in the former discoveries, especially the last, and felt some pain in his ankles at times, but he grew a little better towards night and in time through God's mercy recovered in the use of his means.

January 12th. Friday, we went to work, but about noon it began to rain, so that it forced us to give over work.

This day, two of our people put us in great sorrow and care. There were four sent to gather and cut thatch in the morning, and two of them, John Goodman and Peter Browne, having cut thatch all the forenoon, went to a further place and willed the other two to bind up that which was cut and to follow them. So they did, being about a mile and a half from our plantation. But when the two came after, they could not find them nor hear anything of them at all, though they hallowed and shouted as loud as they could. So they returned to the company and told them of it. Whereupon Master Carver and three or four more went to seek them but could hear nothing of them. So, they returning, sent more; but that night they could hear nothing at all of them. The next day they armed ten or twelve men out, verily thinking the Indians had surprised them. They went seeking

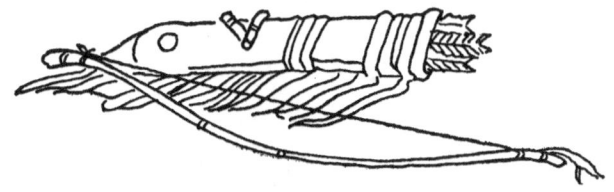

seven or eight miles but could find no trace of them, which much discomforted us all.

The two that were missed, at dinner time took their meat in their hands and would go walk and refresh themselves. So going a little off, they found a lake of water and, having a great mastiff bitch with them and a spaniel, by the water side they found a great deer. The dogs chased him, and they followed so far that they lost themselves and could not find the way back. They wandered all that afternoon, which was wet, and at night it did freeze and snow. They were slenderly apparelled and had no victuals nor any weapons but each one his sickle. They ranged about but could find no shelter.

When it drew to night they were much perplexed, for they could find neither harbor nor meat, but in frost and snow were forced to make the earth their bed and the element their covering. And another thing did very much terrify them. They heard, as they thought, two lions roaring exceedingly for a long time together, and a third that they thought was very near them. So, not knowing what to do,

they resolved to climb up into a tree as their safest refuge. But as that would prove an intolerable cold lodging, they stood at the tree's root, so that when the lions came they might take their opportunity of climbing up. The bitch they were fain to hold by the neck, for she would have been gone to the lion. So they walked up and down under the tree all night, an extreme cold night.

So soon as it was light they traveled again, passing by many lakes and brooks and woods. One place where the savages had burned the ground for the space of five miles in length is fine, even country. In the afternoon, it pleased God that from an high hill they discovered the two isles in the bay. So that night they got to the plantation, being ready to faint with travel and want of victuals, and almost famished with cold. John Goodman was fain to have his shoes cut off his feet, they were so swelled with cold, and it was a long while after ere he was able to go.

Those on the shore were much comforted at their return. But they on ship-board spied their great new rendezvous on fire, which was to them a new discomfort.

Because of the supposed loss of the men, they feared that the savages had fired them. Neither could they presently go to them for want of water. But after three quarters of an hour they went, as they had purposed the day before to keep the Sabbath on the shore, because the greater number of people now was there. At their landing they heard good tidings of the return of the two men, and that the house was fired accidentally by a spark. It flew into the thatch, which instantly burned up, but the roof held and no great hurt. The most loss was Master Carver's and William Bradford's, who then lay sick in bed. If they had not risen with good speed, they had been blown up with powder, but through God's mercy they had no harm. The house was full of beds as close as they could lie one by another, and their muskets were charged, but, blessed by God, there was no harm done.

January 15th. Monday, it rained much all day, so that they on ship-board could not go on shore, nor they on shore do any labor but all were wet.

January 16th, 17th & 18th. Tuesday, Wednesday, and Thursday were very fair sunshiny days, as if it had been in April, and our people, so many as were in health, wrought cheerfully.

January 19th. This day, we resolved to make a shed to put our common provision in, some of which was already set on shore, but at noon it rained, so that we could not work. In the evening John Goodman went abroad to use his lame feet that were pitifully ill with the cold he had got. Having a spaniel with him, a little way off from the plantation two great wolves ran after the dog. The dog ran to him and betwixt his legs for succor. He had nothing in his hand but took up a stick and threw at one of them and hit him. They presently both ran away but came again. He got a pale board in his hand, and they sat both on their tails, grinning at him a good while, then went their way and left him.

January 20th. Saturday, we made up our shed for our common goods.

January 21st. Sunday, we kept our meeting on land.

January 22nd. Monday was a fair day. We wrought on our houses and in the afternoon carried up our hogsheads of meal to our common storehouse.

January 23rd—27th. The rest of the week we followed our business likewise.

January 29th. Monday in the morning there was cold frost and sleet, but afterwards reasonable fair. Both the long boat and the shallop brought our common goods on shore.

January 30th & 31st. Tuesday and Wednesday, it was cold frosty weather and sleet, so that we could not work. In the morning the master and others saw two savages that had been on the island near our ship. What they came for we could not tell, for before they were descried they were gone so far back again that we could not speak with them.

February 4th. Sunday was very wet and rainy with the greatest gusts of wind that ever we had since we came forth. Though we rode in a very good harbor, yet we were in danger because our ship was light and unbalanced, now the goods were taken out. It caused much of the daubing of our houses to fall down.

February 9th. Friday, the cold weather continued still, so that we could do little work. That afternoon our little house for our sick people was set on fire by a spark that kindled in the roof, but no great harm was done. Going ashore that evening, the master killed five geese, which he kindly distributed among the sick people. He found also a good deer killed. The savages had cut off the horns, and a wolf was eating of him. How he came there we could not conceive.

February 16th. Friday was a fair day, but the northerly wind continued, which continued the frost. This afternoon, one of our people being a-fowling, and having taken a stand in the reeds beside a creek about a mile and an half from our plantation, there came by him

twelve Indians marching towards our plantation. In the woods he heard the noise of many more. He lay close till they were passed, and then, with what speed he could, he went home and gave the alarm. So the people abroad in the woods returned and armed themselves. But we saw none of them until toward the evening when they made a great fire about the place where they were first discovered.

Captain Miles Standish and Francis Cooke, being at work in the woods, came home and left their tools behind them. Before they returned their tools were taken away by the savages. This coming of the savages gave us occasion to keep more strict watch and to make our pieces and furniture ready, which by moisture were out of temper.

February 17th. On Saturday in the morning we held a meeting for the enacting of military orders amongst ourselves. We chose Miles Standish our captain and gave him authority of command in affairs. As we were in consultation over it two savages presented themselves upon the top of an hill about a quarter of a mile or less away from our plantation and made signs unto us to come unto them. We in our turn made signs unto them to come to us. Whereupon we armed ourselves and stood ready. We sent two over the brook towards them, to wit: Captain Miles Standish and Stephen Hopkins, who went towards the savages. Only one of our men had a musket, which he laid down in their sight on the ground in sign of peace and to show that we would parley with them. But the savages would not tarry our coming. A noise of a great many more was heard behind the hill, but no more came in sight. This caused us to plant our great ordinances in places most convenient.

February 21st. Wednesday, the master came on shore with many of his sailors. He brought with him one of the great pieces, called a minion, and helped us to draw it up the hill with another piece that lay on shore. We mounted them and a saker and two bases. He brought with him a very fat goose to eat with us, and we had a fat crane and a mallard and a dried neat's tongue. And so we were kindly and friendly together.

March 3rd. Saturday, the wind was south and the morning misty, but towards noon it was warm and fair weather. The birds sang in the woods most pleasantly. At one of the clock it thundered, which was the first we heard in that country. There were strong and great claps, but short. But after an hour it rained very sadly till midnight.

March 7th. Wednesday, the wind was full east, cold but fair. That day Master Carver with five others went to the great ponds, which seem to be excellent fishing places. All the way they went they found it exceedingly beaten and haunted with deer, but they saw none. Amongst other fowl, they saw one milk white fowl with a very black head. This day some garden seeds were sown.

March 16th. Friday was a fair warm day. This morning we determined to conclude of the military orders, which we had begun to consider of before but were interrupted by the savages, as we mentioned formerly. And whilst we were busied here about, we were interrupted again, for there presented himself a savage, which caused an alarm. He very boldly came all alone among the houses and straight towards the rendezvous. We intercepted him there, not suffering him to go in, as undoubtedly he would out of his boldness. He saluted us in English and bade us welcome. He had learned some broken English amongst the Englishmen

that came to fish at Monhegan and knew by name most of the captains, commanders, and masters of the ships which usually come. He was a man free in speech, so far as he was able to express his mind, and of a seemly carriage.

We questioned him of many things, for he was the first savage we could meet with. He said he was not of these parts but of Monhegan and one of the sagamores or lords thereof, Monhegan lying hence a day's sail with a great wind or five days by the land. He had been eight months in these parts.

He discoursed of the whole country and of every province, and of their sagamores and their number of men and strength. The wind beginning to rise a little, we cast a horseman's coat about him, for he was stark naked except for a leather about his waist with a fringe about a span long or a little more. He had a bow and two arrows, one headed and the other unheaded. He was a tall straight man, the hair of his head black, long behind and short before. He had no hair on his face at all. He asked for some beer, but we gave him strong water and biscuit and butter and cheese and pudding and a piece of a mallard. All of these he liked well and had been acquainted with such amongst the English.

He told us the place where we now live is called Patuxet. About four years ago all the inhabitants died of an extraordinary plague. There is neither man, woman, nor child remaining, as indeed we have found none, so that there is none to hinder our possession or to lay claim into it.

All the afternoon we spent in communication with him. We would gladly have been rid of him at night, but he was not willing to go this night. Then we thought to carry him on ship-board, wherewith he was well content and went into the shallop. But the wind was high and the water scant, so that it had to turn back. We lodged him that night at Stephen Hopkins' house and watched him.

March 17th. Saturday in the morning we dismissed the savage after we had given him a knife, a bracelet, and a ring. He promised within a night or two to come again and bring with him some of the Massasoits with such beavers' skins as they had to truck with us. They are our next bordering neighbors and are sixty strong, as he saith. The Nausites are as near Southeast of them and

are a hundred strong. They were those whom our people encountered, as we before related.

They are much incensed and provoked against the English. They slew three Englishmen about eight months ago, and two more hardly escaped by flight to Monhegan. They were Sir Ferdinando Gorge's men, as this savage told us.

He told us likewise of the fight that our discoverers had with the Nausites, and of our tools that were taken out of the woods. We willed him that they should be brought back again, otherwise we would right ourselves. These people are ill affected toward the English by reason of one Hunt, a master of a ship, who deceived them. Under color of trucking with them, he got twenty out of this very place where we inhabit and seven men from the Nausites and carried them away and sold them as slaves for £20 a head, like a wretched man that cares not what mischief he doth for his profit.

March 18th. Sunday was a reasonable fair day. On this day came again the savage and brought with him five other tall proper men. They had every man a deer's skin on him, and the principal of them had a wildcat's skin or such like on one arm. Most of them had long hose up to their groins, close made, and above their groins to their waist another leather, altogether like Irish trousers. They are of complexion like our English Gypsies with no hair or very little on their faces. On their heads they have long hair to their shoulders, only cut before, some trussed up with a feather broadwise like a fan, others with a fox tail hanging out.

According to our charge, these left their bows and arrows a quarter of a mile from our town. We gave them entertainment as we thought was fitting them. They did eat liberally of our English victuals and made semblance unto us of friendship and amity. They sang and danced after their manner like clowns. In a thing like a bowcase, which the principal of them had about his waist, they brought with them a little of their corn pounded to powder, which they put with a little water and eat. He had a little tobacco in a bag, but none of them smoked but when he listed. Some of them had their faces painted black from the forehead to the chin, four or five fingers broad; others after other fashions, as they liked.

They brought three or four skins, but we would not truck with them at all that day, but wished them to bring more and we would truck for all. They promised to return within a night or two and would leave these skins behind, though we were not willing they should. They brought us all our tools again, which had been taken in the woods in our men's absence.

And so, because of the day, we dismissed them so soon as we could. When we sent them from us, we took care to give every one of them some little trifles, especially the principals among them. We carried them along with our arms to the place where they left their bows and arrows, whereat they were amazed. Two of them began to slink away, but another called him, and they took their arrows. We bade them farewell, and they were glad. And so, with many thanks given us, they departed with promise they would come again. But Samoset, our first acquaintance, either was sick or feigned himself so and would not go with them but stayed with us.

March 19th & 20th. Monday and Tuesday proved fair days. We digged our grounds and sowed our garden seeds.

March 21st. Wednesday was a fine warm day. We dispatched Samoset to them to know the reason they came not according to their words. We gave him an hat, a pair of stockings and shoes, a short, and a piece of cloth to tie about his waist.

That day we had again a meeting to conclude of laws and orders for ourselves and to confirm those military orders that were formerly propounded and twice broken off by

the savages' coming. But so we were again interrupted the third time, for, after we had been an hour together, on the top of the hill over against us two or three savages presented themselves and made semblance of daring us, as we thought. So Captain Standish and another with their muskets went over to them, and two of the master's mates followed them without arms. The savages whetted and rubbed their arrows and strings to make show of defiance, but when our men drew near they ran away. Thus we were again interrupted by them. This day with much ado we got our carpenter, who had been long sick of the scurvy, to fit our shallop to fetch all from aboard.

March 22nd. Thursday was a very fair warm day. About noon we met again on our public business but had scarce been an hour together when Samoset came again with three others and Squanto, a native of Patuxet where we now inhabit. He was one of the twenty captives who were carried away by Hunt. He had been in England and dwelt in Corn-hill with master John Slany, a merchant, and could speak a little English. They brought with them some few skins to truck and some red herrings newly taken and dried, but not salted.

They signified unto us that their great sagamore, Massasoit, was hard by with Quadequina, his brother, and all their men. They could not well express in English what they would, but after an hour the king with sixty men in his train came to the top of an hill over against us, so that we could well behold them. They were unwilling to come to us, so Squanto went again unto them.

He brought back word that we should send one to parley with them. We sent Edward Winslow to know their mind and to signify the mind and will of our governor, which was to have trading and peace with them. We sent to the king a pair of knives and a copper chain with a jewel at it. To Quadequina we sent likewise a knife and a jewel to hang in his ear, and withal a pot of strong water, a good quantity of biscuit, and some butter, which were all willingly accepted.

Our messenger made a speech unto him, saying that King James saluted him with words of love and peace and did accept of him as his friend and ally, and that our governor desired to see him and to truck with him and to confirm a peace with him as his next neighbor. He liked well the speech and heard it attentively, though the interpreters did not well express it. After he had eaten and drunk and given the rest to his company, he looked upon the sword and armor which our man had on with intimation of his desire to

buy it. But on the other side our messenger showed his unwillingness to part with it. In the end the king left him in the custody of Quadequina, his brother, and came over the brook with some twenty men who left all their bows and arrows behind. We kept six or seven of them as hostages for our messenger.

Captain Standish and Master Williamson met the king at the brook with half a dozen musketeers. They saluted him and he them, and so, one going to the other side of the brook to him, one on one side of it and the other on the other side conducted him to an house then in building. There we placed a green rug and three or four cushions. Then instantly came our governor with drum and trumpet after him and some few musketeers. After salutations, our governor kissed his hand and the king kissed him and so they sat down. The governor called for some strong water and drunk to him, and Massasoit drunk a great draught that made him sweat

all the while after. The governor called for a little fresh meat, which the king did eat willingly and did give his followers. Then they treated of peace, which was:

1. That neither he nor any of his should injure or do hurt to any of our people.

2. And if any of his did hurt to any of ours, he should send the offender, that we might punish him.

3. That if any of our tools were taken away when our people were at work, he should cause them to be restored; and if ours did any harm to any of his, we would do the like to them.

4. If any did unjustly war against him, we would aid him; if any did war against us, he should aid us.

5. He should send to his neighbor confederates to certify them of this, that they might not wrong us but might be likewise comprised in the conditions of peace.

6. That when their men came to us they should leave their bows and arrows behind them, as we should do our pieces when we came to them.

Lastly, that doing thus, King James would esteem of him as his friend and ally.

All this the king seemed to like well, and it was applauded of his followers. All the while he sat by the governor he trembled for fear. In his person he is a very lusty man in his best years, an able body, grave of countenance, and spare of speech. In his attire he differs little or nothing from the rest of his followers, only in a great chain of white bone beads about his neck. At it behind his neck hangs a little bag of tobacco, which he smoked and gave us to smoke. His face was painted with a deep red like mulberry, and he was oiled both head and face so that he looked greasily. All his followers' faces likewise were in part or in whole painted, some black, some red, some yellow, some white, and some with crosses and other antic works. Some had skins on them and some were naked; all were strong, tall men in appearance.

So after all was done, the governor conducted him to the brook, and there they embraced each other and he departed. We diligently kept our hostages, expecting our messenger's coming, but anon word was brought us that

Quadequina was coming, and our messenger was stayed till his return. He presently came and a troupe with him, so we likewise entertained him and conveyed him to the place prepared. He was very fearful of our pieces and made signs of dislike and that they should be carried away, whereupon commandment was given they should be laid away.

He was a proper, tall, young man of a modest and seemly countenance, and he did like our entertainment kindly. We conveyed him back likewise as we did the king, but divers of their people stayed. Then, as soon as he had returned, they dismissed our messenger, who returned safely to us.

Two of his people would have stayed all night, but we would not suffer it. One thing I forgot, the king had in his bosom hanging on a string a great long knife. He marvelled much at our trumpet, and some of his men would sound it as well as they could. Samoset and Squanto remained all night with us, but the king and all his men lay all night in the woods. They were not above half an English mile from us and had all their wives and women with them. They said that within eight or nine days they would come and set corn on the other side of the brook which is hard by us and dwell there all summer. That night we kept good watch, but there was no appearance of danger.

March 23rd. The next morning divers of their people came over to us, hoping to get some victuals as we imagined. Some of them told us the king would have some of us come see him. Captain Standish and Isaac Allerton went venturously and were welcomed by him after his

manner. He gave them three or four ground nuts and some tobacco.

We cannot yet conceive but that he is willing to have peace with us. They have seen our people in the woods sometimes two or three alone at work and fowling and have offered them no harm, as they might easily have done. And we are especially encouraged to believe this because he hath a potent adversary, the Narragansetts, that are at war with him. Against these he thinks we may be some strength to him, for our pieces are terrible unto them.

This morning they stayed till ten or eleven of the clock. Our governor bid them send the king's kettle, and we filled it full of peas, which pleased them well. And so they went their way.

Friday was a very fair day. Samoset and Squanto still remained with us. Squanto went at noon to fish for eels and at night came home with as many as he could well lift in one hand, which our people were glad of. They were fat and sweet. He trod them out with his feet and so caught them with his hands without any other instrument.

This day we proceeded on with our common business, from which we had been so often hindered by the savages' coming. We concluded both of military orders and of some laws and orders as we thought behooveful for our present estate and condition, and did likewise choose our governor for this year, which was Master John Carver, a man well approved amongst us.

www.ingramcontent.com/pod-product-compliance
Lightning Source LLC
LaVergne TN
LVHW041629070526
838199LV00052B/3288